2/11

Date Due		

High School Musicals™

SCENERY and SET DESIGN

rosen publishing's
rosen central®

New York

Diane Bailey

Published in 2010 by The Rosen Publishing Group, Inc.
29 East 21st Street, New York, NY 10010

First Edition

Library of Congress Cataloging-in-Publication Data

Bailey, Diane, 1966–
Scenery and set design / Diane Bailey.—1st ed.
    p. cm.—(High school musicals)
Includes bibliographical references and index.
ISBN-13: 978-1-4358-5257-0 (library binding)
ISBN-13: 978-1-4358-5528-1 (pbk)
ISBN-13: 978-1-4358-5529-8 (6 pack)
1. Musicals—Stage guides. I. Title.
MT955.B18 2009
792.6'4—dc22
                        2008040861

Manufactured in Malaysia

Contents

INTRODUCTION

Beauty and the Beast. Yes, there's a musical with that name. It is also a good way to describe the scenery of a musical. Elaborate scenery is beautiful to look at—but it can be beastly to make!

Think of the helicopter that lands onstage in the final scenes of *Miss Saigon*. The sinking of the larger-than-life *Titanic*. The chandelier that falls through the house and crashes onstage in *The Phantom of the Opera*.

Audiences remember those spectacular stunts. And the people who thought them up and made them work? They remember the incredibly hard work it took to get them onstage.

Sometimes, things go wrong. In a London production of *Mary Poppins*, the complex sets broke down. The show had to stop while the crew repaired them. A law said that child actors had to leave

People are fascinated by the story of the *Titanic*, the massive ocean liner that sank in 1912. For this Broadway production, scenery designers captured the audience's attention with a set that re-created the sinking ship.

the theater by 11 PM. Because of the delay, the children in the show missed their final scene. (The actor playing their dad stuffed pillows in their beds and pretended they were asleep.)

Other times, it's not the sets that are at fault. The morning that the play *Golda* was supposed to open in New York in 1974, a fire tore through the theater, destroying the entire set. The production quickly moved to a new theater, and *Golda* opened as scheduled— minus the sets. Audiences didn't seem to care that there wasn't any scenery, and the play was a hit.

This doesn't mean that scenery is undesirable! Elaborate sets may not always be required, but they can make things more interesting. People have long enjoyed adding "extras" to the necessities. They still print slogans on T-shirts and put ketchup on their fries. The same goes for beautiful scenery added to a good show. The end result is that much more satisfying.

On Broadway, the sets are sometimes the star of the show. At *Glengarry Glen Ross*, for example, the audience was so impressed that they gave the sets a standing ovation. A set designer can take theatergoers to another world, and they don't even have to leave their seats—except, of course, when they stand to applaud.

Setting the Stage

What is the most important thing for creating great sets? A competent crew? Lots of money? Actually, a set designer's best friend is something much more available: imagination. The set designer uses his or her own imagination to create sets. Then, the set designer depends on the audience's imagination to fill in the blanks.

Creating a Look

If you ask a typical audience member what scenery does, he or she might say that it provides a background for the play. It establishes a sense of time and place. Scenery is eye candy that helps spin the magic of the theater.

If that's the role of scenery, then sets do something a little different. Their job is more practical. On the most basic level, they give the actors somewhere to go (or not to go). They create areas on the stage,

A cutout of a gondola is enough to take audience members to an exotic setting in this London production of Gilbert and Sullivan's *The Gondoliers.*

and they hide backstage areas that the audience should not see. Part of a set designer's job is to make sure that sets and scenery work together.

Sets and scenery help set the mood of a production for audience members. *Les Misérables* will be a serious production. *Seussical: The Musical* will be zany and fun. Good scenery will reflect those different moods. Set designers consider what the musical is about. Then, they find a way to make a statement. They might emphasize a couple of objects or places that are important in the musical. They might use a specific color palette. Dark colors and heavy objects often fit the mood of a tragedy. A comedy will be brighter and have amusing details. Suppose you need to create a forest. You might choose to make individual cutout trees, like in a cartoon. Or, you could paint a cloth in subtle greens and browns. Both are outdoor scenes, but they feel very different.

Will your sets be elaborate or simple? The budget will affect some decisions. However, a simple set that depends on one or two elements can be just as powerful as a set with lots of details.

Set designer James Korf gave an interview to Calvin College's *Spark* magazine. He said, "The art of set design is at its highest when it is not noticed. If someone says 'Great costumes,' or 'Did you see those lights?' that's a bad thing. Those impressions should all happen on a non-verbal level."

In Shakespeare's time, plays had few sets—or none. The audience had to pay attention to the dialogue, costumes, and props. From those, they could figure out where and when the play

The Globe Theatre in London is a replica of the original theater, which was built in 1599 by the theater company of England's most famous playwright—William Shakespeare.

took place. Minimalist scenery works best in shows that have only a few settings. These shows depend more on the emotional content of the play. Musicals usually need something fancier. However, that does not mean you can't take a few shortcuts.

When you are working on a high school show, chances are you won't have enough money or time to create elaborate sets for every scene. Pick the scenes that matter, and concentrate your efforts on them. You may focus on a set that can be used in several different scenes. By making a few changes, a set can become a whole other place, even though its basic structure is the same. Or,

Smart Sets

At some theaters, designers use virtual reality scenery. "Virtual reality" means using computers to create a situation and setting. Then, a person interacts with this new "reality." It is similar to a video game. The setting is created in advance, but what the player does can change each time. The actors practice during rehearsal to see how they best interact with the virtual sets.

In one show, designers used the technology to show how the characters' thoughts were far away from their bodies. The actors' shadows were captured by the computer and projected to stay in one place—hard at work at their desks. Meanwhile, the actual people got up and walked around. In another scene, an actor performed from offstage, through a video camera. The computer made his image get bigger and bigger throughout his speech. Offstage, of course, his real body stayed the same size!

you may spend your energy on a set that is used a limited number of times—maybe only once! But, because it's so important to the show, it will have a big impact.

Set Requirements

"Built to last." When it comes to houses and furniture, people generally want to buy something that is not going to fall apart. The same holds true for sets. After all, you do not want your heroine to tumble off the balcony. However, there is a key difference between set building and other types of construction. In most cases, sets are made to be temporary. They will be broken down at the end of a show.

Sets may have a relatively short life, but that does not mean they can be poorly constructed. They must hold up even through the demands of an active show. Sets and stage furniture often must be sturdier than the same objects are in real life. For example, your musical may include dancing on the table. That's not something you would do in your own dining room—at least not night after night. So, the first requirement for a set is to be safe and structurally sound.

For example, there are certain steps involved in building a flat. A flat is a type of set that looks like a giant picture frame, but there's more to it. A piece of wood called a toggle goes horizontally across the middle, holding the sides of the frame straight. The toggle attaches to the frame with a keystone, another block of wood that adds strength. Braces are placed diagonally within the frame. Sometimes, a corner block (shaped like a triangle) is fitted into the corner to add stability. By taking these steps, the builders make sure the flat won't fall apart during heavy use.

11

Experienced set builders have all the basics on hand: hammers, rulers, and ample working space.

Now, consider that the crew has to move all this stuff around. Better make sure it is not too heavy or awkward. It must be portable. The set may look as permanent as the Grand Canyon, but it may have to disappear in thirty seconds.

As if that wasn't enough pressure, set builders are asked to add a couple of other factors into the mix. For one thing, they've got to

be fast. If rehearsals run six weeks, then the set builders have five weeks to get the sets onstage in time for technical rehearsals. They are also expected to make things inexpensively. Some professional productions will have large budgets, but everyone—even the big guys— works within some kind of budget. Good builders will look for ways to save money. After all, they may need those pennies for another part of the set that goes over budget.

Working with the Director and Design Team

Every musical has a certain style and personality. The set designer works closely with the director to make sure that personality shows

Money Matters

Although you may not be in charge of the budget, it's a good idea to look for ways to cut costs. Think outside of the box. Is it necessary to build a brand-new set, or can you adapt what you already have? How can you build a piece so that it can do several things? If you don't have something you need, and you can't afford to build it, how else can you get it? Look around for "found objects" that might work. John Kaluta is a high school teacher who has helped stage many shows. In his book *The Perfect Stage Crew*, he tells the story of how he donated the front door of his house for the three-week run of one musical.

Find out if parents, teachers, or local businesses can help. They might be able to donate scrap lumber or leftover paint. You might borrow pieces from another school or community theater. If you need something unusual, put out a call through the student newspaper or school newsletter. You never know what you might turn up. Plus, you'll get a little publicity for your show!

through. They discuss the overall idea of the show. They identify what the mood and the tone are. Then, they decide what "look" will work best. The first clue will be the musical itself. Is it a serious, even tragic story, such as *Les Misérables*? A light comedy, such as *Thoroughly Modern Millie*? Or, does it have elements of both? Meeting with the director helps to establish the creative approach.

Now, the set designer must consider the technical aspects. How exactly will the set be built and installed? Professional shows have a technical director. This person is in charge of the set designer, the lighting director, the sound director, and the costume people. In high school, the technical director might also be the director of the

A simple bedroom set provides the backdrop for rehearsing actors. Having set pieces—or at least placeholders—onstage helps get actors used to moving around the set.

play or the stage manager. It might be the set designer. Whoever it is, the set designer will work with this person to make sure the set actually works on a practical level.

Remember to keep your perspective. It is easy to get caught up in details. You might get so excited about the design of a complicated set that you forget how important it is in the whole scheme of things. Take time to step back, look at the big picture, and make sure you are on track.

The Raw Materials

The hammer and paintbrush are ready, and it is tempting to get straight to work. However, there is something you have to do before you start to build, decorate, or even imagine a piece of scenery. First, you have to know what its purpose is.

Read the Script

The playwright wrote the script, the director chose it, and the actors have to perform it. The set designer doesn't need to memorize lines, but it's still necessary to read the script, even if you think you know it already. In fact, you should probably read it a couple of times.

The first time through, read the play for enjoyment, but pay attention to the impressions it gives you. Does it make you laugh? Is there a sense of fear? Do you have any physical reactions? If you could choose words to describe it, what would they be? Intimate or

The comfort of home is the only set needed for a designer's first step: reading the script and becoming familiar with the play.

grand? Bright or dark? Highly realistic or somewhat magical? It's the set designer's job to find the feelings in the script and translate them into something concrete: the set.

In old movies, it was common for the good guy to ride a white horse and for the bad guy to have a black one. You may want to capitalize on obvious connections like those, or you may decide to turn the whole thing on its head.

You'll also want to keep track of other things that will affect set design and building. How many different scenes are there, and how many sets do those require? How often do the scenes change? Will the actors need to move quickly between two or three different scenes—for example, the inside of a restaurant out onto the street? Or, from a cozy bedroom into the wild woods beyond? Keep in mind how one set can transition into the next one. If a scene change comes at an exciting point in the production, think about how your set can change without slowing down the action.

Also pay attention to stage directions. Sometimes, the script will include instructions like "Mary picks up the glass and walks across the room." As the set designer, you'll want to make sure nothing is in Mary's way during her walk.

However, the script might be more subtle. Perhaps Mary says, "I can't stand being inside! Look out there! It's a beautiful day." If Mary was lying down on her bed, she probably had to throw back her covers, get up, and walk to the window to indicate the beautiful day. What does that mean for the set designer? He'll need a set that includes a window, with a view of a beautiful day beyond. If Mary is really committed to getting out of the house, she may fling open the door and go outside. That means the door built into the set must be practical—it must actually work like a door, not simply be a picture of one.

Do Your Research

Scenery helps an audience sink into the magic of the production, so make sure your scenery doesn't accidentally yank them right back out. Most musicals have a strong sense of place. There's Paris during the French Revolution in *Les Misérables*. *Brigadoon* takes place in the highlands of Scotland. The savannah comes to life in *The Lion King*.

Scenery, props, and costumes work together to bring authenticity to period pieces—plays that take place during a certain historical time.

Good scenery will evoke the feel of these places. Bad scenery might ruin the experience. Clean, well-lit streets don't fit the seedy side of Paris. Palm trees don't grow in Scotland. Parrots don't live in dry Africa. Avoid making mistakes by doing some research about the musical. Figure out where it's set and when. Then, find out what that place looked like. How tall were the buildings? What shape were the windows? Is the landscape woody or barren? What sort of dishes did people use? Did the women wear long skirts? Did the men have long hair?

Costumes and props will often be handled by other people in the production. However, the more you know about the time and place of your show, the better your scenery will be. Also, costumes and props might affect how you design your sets. For example, a musical might have a dance number with a dozen women wearing bulky dresses. You need to make sure they have enough room to maneuver without playing bumper-skirts.

It's helpful to keep scrapbooks and sketchbooks, especially if you are interested in set design as a career. Recording your ideas as you go along will help you remember them. Also, you'll have your own personal library of swatches and samples.

Know Your Stage

Stages come in a variety of shapes, sizes, and layouts. The most common is the proscenium. This stage basically forms a box, with an opening called the proscenium arch. Think of a shoebox diorama. That will give you a good idea what a proscenium stage looks like. This type of stage divides the stage from the house. The imaginary "fourth wall" is the line that runs between the actors and the audience. Most high schools will probably have a proscenium theater. The part of the stage in front of the proscenium arch is called the apron. Because the proscenium stage separates the audience from the stage, this type of stage works best for elaborate sets and effects.

Another kind of stage is the thrust stage. It pokes out into the audience, like a peninsula. The audience sits around the stage on three sides. In-the-round stages are like islands. The audience completely surrounds the stage. Thrust and in-the-round stages are more intimate. The audience is often closer to the performers and can see from different angles. However, there are fewer places to position scenery without blocking the audience's view. It is also trickier to move scenery on and off. In-the-round theaters depend heavily on two directions—up and down. Scenery goes up into the "flies," or down into "traps" below the stage. With these types of stages, using light and sound to create effects is even more important.

The Floor

Don't ignore the floor. In most theaters, the audience will see more of the floor than anything else. You might be able to paint all or parts of the floor to make it more attractive. Or, you might add some kind of covering. However, in a musical that requires a lot of dancing, be sure not to use a covering that might make the dancers trip, such as a loose carpet. Using platforms to add levels to the stage is another way to create points of interest. Also, remember that the stage floor will probably be taped to indicate where certain sets are placed or where actors will walk. This tape may show up under the lights, so be sure not to use too much!

Audience and Actors

Scenery is no good if no one can see it. Before any set is built—or even drawn—it's necessary to know where the audience's sightlines are. Go sit in the extreme left and right seats in the very first row of the house, as well as in the very back row. Occasionally, it won't

With stairs, chairs, and a busy background, the set designer for this high school production in Poughkeepsie, New York, had to take into account how several actors would navigate around the set.

be the first or last row that has the farthest-out seats. Wherever they are, go find them. If there's a balcony, do the same up there. Sketch out how much is visible. Now you know what the audience can see.

Sets mostly affect what the audience sees or doesn't see. However, they also influence the sound. For example, some sets might need to have speakers hidden behind them or inside of them. They might also influence how sound travels around the stage.

Your other concern is the actors. The sets have to work for them as well. Two imaginary lines bisect the stage. The center line runs right down the center of the stage, from upstage to downstage, perpendicular to an audience row. The plaster line is horizontal, parallel to the audience, and is just upstage of the proscenium arch. Most action of the play will radiate from the point where these two lines cross.

That's not to say everything will happen there—of course it won't. But think of it as "home base" for the actors. Use it to figure out how the actors will be moving around. Then, decide which parts of the stage can have sets on them and which parts need to remain clear.

Sets and scenery also influence how and where the actors make their entrances and exits. They create focal points. These

Curtains

In addition to creating an illusion of place and time, a set has a more humble job, too. It "masks" (hides) offstage areas. Most theaters have several curtains that can be used for this purpose. The curtains may move from side to side, like the ones in most homes, or up and down, like window shades. Most theater curtains are made of black or dark-colored velvet or velour. These plush, dark fabrics absorb light.

Curtains that are located above the stage, and hide the upper workings of the theater, are called borders. Curtains that hang down, at the sides of the stage, are called legs. Sometimes, borders are called teasers, and legs are called tormentors. It's possible to use the curtains as design elements in your set. In one show, the legs were dressed to look like actual, gigantic legs. Curtains can be as useful as you need them to be, with just a little creativity!

focal points invite the audience members to concentrate on a particular area of the stage. You can think of the stage as being divided into three separate sections—left, right, and center. In general, you will want to keep the middle area of the stage clear for the action of the play.

3
CHAPTER

Designing the Set

You've got a good feel for the musical. You've got a good idea how your stage is going to help or limit you. Now, it's time to play matchmaker and make the two work together.

Types of Sets

You don't want the performances to be flat, but fortunately, the sets can be. Ever since the days of the ancient Greeks, "flats" have been the basis for most sets. A flat isn't truly flat—that only exists in the imaginary world of geometry! However, it is only a few inches thick. It's a frame, often made of wood but sometimes of plastic or lightweight metal. This frame is usually covered in cloth, such as canvas. The canvas is then painted or otherwise decorated to represent virtually anything—from a bedroom wall to a vast prairie landscape. Flats may also have doors and windows cut into them.

A set builder works to secure the interior bracing of a large flat. These cross pieces will ensure the flat does not twist or break.

Flats are easy to construct, move, and store, so they can easily make up the main parts of a set.

To add another layer to the scene, or to change it quickly, a "drop" may be the answer. These large, painted cloths hang above the stage and drop down. They are weighted at the bottom so they don't snag or tangle on the way.

Different kinds of cloth can be used to give different effects. For example, a "scrim" changes its look depending on the lighting.

When the lights are shining on it from the front, the scrim is opaque. The audience sees whatever is painted on the cloth, but they can't see what's behind it. Now, bring down those front lights and pull up the ones behind the scrim. The view changes. The audience can see through the cloth to the action that is happening behind it. With a little lighting magic, the stage crew can create two different scenes without ever moving anything!

Platforms take the action to a new level—literally. For example, a character may walk upstairs to her bedroom or out onto the balcony. Keep in mind that a platform must be strong enough to bear the performers' weight. Complicated sets are sometimes put on top of "wagons," or "trucks." These wheeled platforms make it easy to move the set. Many theaters have a cyclorama that covers the whole back of the stage. The cyclorama, or "cyc," resembles a large movie screen. It may be made of cloth or other material, but it's smooth and neutral-colored, so it can be lit in a variety of ways.

Three Sides to Every Issue

In the plays of the ancient Greeks, the characters were sometimes two-faced—and the sets were three-faced. Periaktoi are one of the most ancient types of sets. Think of a "triangle tube"—a triangle stretched out to have three sides and two ends. The periaktoi stood on one end. Then, each of the three sides was painted to represent one of three different types of theater: comedy, tragedy, and satire. Several periaktoi were lined up to create a scene. When the action changed, the panels were simply swiveled onto a new side.

The Elements of Design

Visual designs are made up of several different elements. For example, there are color, texture, line, weight, and space. A designer's style and attitude comes from how he or she uses these elements.

A designer will consider several options. How will sets and furniture be arranged? How will the sets direct the audience's eye? What space will they take up? What will they leave empty?

Strong lines make this eye-catching set work well with the dramatic movements of the actors.

Consider the audience's viewpoint. Remember that sets don't have to be completely realistic. If it suits the overall mood of the musical, then you could try playing around with perspective and balance. Suppose you have a man at work at his desk. If the desk is far too big for him, it might give the impression that his job is overwhelming. If it is too small, you can give the idea that he's too big for the job.

The stark contrast between the girl in white and the dark silhouette next to her shows how form and light can make even a simple set quite powerful.

Once the form of the sets and scenery are in place, start working in the details that will give it its final look. Color is probably the biggest factor at work. Will you use a primary-color palette of blue, red, and yellow? Or, does the show ask for a tropical mix of orange and green? Maybe it cries out for an overtone of blue-black mystery or shimmering purple.

Add texture to your sets as well. One easy trick is to mix sawdust with the paint to give it a rougher appearance. (Your set builders should have plenty of sawdust to spare!)

Light It Up

No set will show up on a dark stage. The art of lighting probably started as a way to make sure that the audience could see the stage and that the actors didn't fall off it.

Lighting has since evolved into a wonderful tool for

the set designer. Flood something in a red light and the effect is totally different than if it's washed in blue. Designers can use spotlights to highlight areas or strobes to create an active look. In general, a set with lots of detail needs only simple lighting. A spare, uncluttered set requires lighting that is more dramatic.

Set designer Derek McLane summed it up in an interview with the online magazine *CurtainUp*. "So much modern scenery is about how you light it. Many plays are written with 20–40 scenes and you really can't make all those places with hard physical scenery," he said. "You're dependent upon creating a lot of those places with light and color and shapes."

Projections are another way to create scenery. With them, you don't ever have to drive a nail or dip a paintbrush. Projections can be a way to create something complicated or exotic. All you need is a screen and a projector, right? Well, yes, but it's not quite that easy. For projections to look good, you may need a computer program that will let you control the images. So, you may have to buy software. You will also need someone who knows how to use it.

Also, projections are only as good as the surface onto which they are displayed. If your surface is bumpy or discolored, the image will suffer. Also, theaters are large, and the projections have to reach a long way. The "throw" of the image will be distorted over long distances. Finally, make sure your performers do not walk through the beams of light. Otherwise, your gorgeous landscape might temporarily disappear!

Moving effects, such as rain, are ideal to make with projections. Perhaps you have a character who must struggle through a blinding snowstorm. Or, perhaps he is daydreaming, gazing at the clouds floating overhead. In those cases, projections can be effective— and your stage will stay dry.

Using Furniture

Don't jump on the bed! At home, furniture is meant to be treated kindly, at least a little. But stage furniture has a whole different set of rules. The actors may jump on the bed, dance on the table, or throw a chair across the room. It may be necessary to shore up existing furniture so it can take this extra "action," or it may even be necessary to build something special.

Another thing to consider when choosing furniture is to make sure it doesn't slow the action. If your hero must leap up in surprise, he may not want to start from the bottom of a large, overstuffed chair. If your heroine is dressed in an enormous hoop skirt, she may not be able to get up at all without help! Large, cushy furniture pieces may dwarf the actors. But do not compensate by using too many smaller pieces, or else you may clutter up the stage. Two chairs can give the impression of a living room just as well as a multipiece sectional couch.

Take Stock of the Stock

Many theaters keep an inventory of stock scenery. This is scenery that has been used in previous plays and is kept on hand to use again. Stock is usually made up of flat scenery, which is easy to store. It may also include complicated pieces that are difficult to build, such as stairs.

Modern musicals can be challenging for designers. The shows might be set in an elaborate or even fantastical place. Also, audiences are used to seeing amazing effects on television or at the movies. That puts more pressure on designers. They may want to come up with cool tricks inside the theater as well.

Unless you have a huge budget, this is not always practical. You can use some stock scenery to save money and time. Of

The lines of ladders and the colors of painted flats make this scenery storage area look like a work of art itself.

course, you do not have to use a piece exactly as you find it. For example, you might have a staircase that is painted to look like the battered steps outside an apartment building. You can redecorate it so that you have a carpeted staircase that will fit perfectly into a grand mansion. It looks different, but the stairs underneath are the same. They will still get the actors upstairs.

Inexperienced designers and builders may be too eager to use the stock as is. Be sure not to let the choice of stock scenery dictate what you do. If it doesn't fit the production, see if you can make it fit. If not, then don't use it. It is better to use something simpler—or even nothing at all—than a piece that is all wrong.

Building a Set

Imagine trying to drive across the country without a map. You might get there eventually, but it would take a lot longer and you'd waste a lot of gas. Planning your route ahead of time is important. In the case of set design, you should have several "maps" in your glove compartment. These will show you what your set pieces will look like and where they will go on the stage. They will also give your set builders the instructions they need to take ideas and turn them into actual structures.

The Paper Trail

Your first step will probably be drawing a ground plan. This is a diagram that gives a bird's-eye view of the stage. Sets and furniture are drawn on it to show their placement. The idea is to know where everything goes. That way, you can make sure that all the pieces fit and that the actors have enough room to move around.

The black, white, and red color scheme of this model, along with its bold checkerboard floor, gives this designer a preview of how the finished set will look.

An elevation drawing shows the sets from another angle. Instead of looking down, imagine that you are looking straight forward. This drawing gives a detailed vertical view. For example, you might be looking at the side of a building. The elevation will show how high the roof is, where the window starts, and what kind of trim surrounds the door. It might even show the style of doorknob or the type of flowers in the window box.

Some parts of the set may be particularly complex. A detail view will give a close-up of these areas. Finally, "renderings" are perspective drawings. They give the impression of a three-dimensional view of the stage.

Construction drawings are also called working drawings. These give instructions about how to build a set piece. These drawings might show a cutaway view, where an object is sliced open to reveal the inside. This helps the builders understand how it fits together.

Although you may not create all of these drawings, it's a good idea to do as much as you can on paper (or the computer) before you start to build. Then, you can see where things might go wrong.

For complicated sets, you might choose to build a model. Sometimes, it's hard to visualize exactly how something will look. Will the stairs be too tall or too short? Will that oversized car be larger-than-life or just plain too large? A model can give you a more realistic idea of how the set will actually look and feel.

To make a model, construct a box that is a scale ratio of your stage. Professionals usually use a black, matte-finish board to do this. Then, using white board, build the sets and furniture. If you can, make your model in black and white first. This will make it easier to spot any problems in size or scale. Later, you can add in color and other details to get a fuller picture for the overall design.

It's also a good idea to add a couple of people to your model. Everyone immediately understands the human form. There's no better way to give a feel for the scale of the set.

Construction and Painting

Most sets are built from wood. Wood is sturdy, inexpensive, and widely available. Often, softwoods like pine are used. Plywood and pressboard are other choices. Other sets may use metal,

Pencils Down, Please

Many professional designers use CAD (computer-aided drawing) software. With CAD, you do not have to spend time sharpening pencils or cleaning up smudges. The computer will not make any mistakes in measuring. Your drawings will be perfectly accurate. These programs create three-dimensional images from any angle. You can try out new color schemes, experiment with different textures, or change the size of certain elements. Best of all, you do everything with just a few mouse clicks.

CAD programs have drawbacks as well. They usually cost a lot of money. They can also be very complicated to use. For a professional designer, it is often worth the time to learn how to use them. However, it can take months or years to become really good. You may not have time during the course of one show to make it worthwhile. Also, some designers say they are most creative when they do things the old-fashioned way. They like having a pencil and sketchbook—and maybe an eraser or two.

plastic, cardboard, or foam. Luan is one popular material. This soft, lightweight, and inexpensive plywood is made from a mix of tropical woods. It is not strong enough for structural use and is hard to paint, but it works well for filler or light bracing. You will need to determine how the piece will be used and then choose the best material. Talk to the director and to the adult in charge of the scene shop to make the best decision.

Flats are usually built by putting together a wooden frame and then covering it with a painted cloth, such as canvas. However, what if the script calls for the actor to kick the wall? Canvas won't withstand that. Instead, you may need to use plywood. Now, the set can take the abuse, but it will be heavier. You will have to consider that when planning scene changes.

Many sets include more than one piece. They fit together (and come apart) at places called break points. Make sure that the look of the design, as well as any practical considerations, work with the break points.

A sure hand and an eye for color are good qualities for scene painters, such as this woman working on a Florida production of *Cinderella*.

When it comes time to paint and decorate your sets, remember that the stage is different from the scene shop. Try to test how your painted sets look onstage under various lighting conditions. Take note of whether the paint dries darker or lighter.

Set decoration is its own art form. Sets are meant to be seen from the first row of the theater and the last, which might be a hundred feet away. When it comes time to paint, be bold.

Don't Break a Leg

Theater people tell actors to "Break a leg." Of course, that is just an expression. Unfortunately, theater can be risky business, even if you are not onstage.

Scene shops are often accidents waiting to happen. There are risks on top of every ladder and inside every

Setting Up Shop

Before you can build, you need a space to build. If possible, choose a central location that is easy for everyone to get to. That way, you can share tools and keep up with design changes. You can spot problems earlier and work together to solve them. If your high school offers technical classes in carpentry or metalworking, you might be able to use those workshops and supplies. If not, you might be doing some of the work in garages or basements.

A good scene shop will be equipped with a variety of tools and materials, large and small. You'll need hammers, nails, saws, pliers, files, screwdrivers, drills, wrenches, measuring tools—the list goes on. If people lend their own tools, be sure to label them with the person's name. If you need special equipment, a local carpenter might share his or her tools—and maybe his or her knowledge.

paint can. However, you can take basic steps to stay safe. Here are some tips:

- Wear protective clothing and gear where appropriate, such as gloves and goggles.
- Make sure the area is well ventilated.
- Keep things neat and clearly labeled.
- Make sure there is running water nearby, as well as a first-aid kit.
- Know what to do in case of an emergency.
- Do not rush.
- Do not work alone—always have a buddy in case of an accident.

Creating this detailed border requires one man working on a ladder—and two more on the ground to help.

- Do not work when you are tired or when anything else might affect your judgment (such as taking medication).
- Do not overwork to prove you are "dedicated."
- Do not do things you don't know how to do (and don't let others).
- Do not ignore the rules. Posted signs and directions from the director or teachers are there for a reason.

If you survived the building of the sets without injury, that's an accomplishment. Now, you have to make sure that no one gets hurt during the actual show. A theater stage is not well-suited to safety. You've got the cast and crew hurrying around. The spaces may be as dark, twisty, and cramped as the bowels of the theater in *Phantom of the Opera*. Actors might be wearing bulky clothing. The crew may be struggling with heavy pieces that don't stay in one place.

There is lots of stuff underfoot. And it's not only at their feet: the airspace above is cluttered with ropes, cables, curtains, cloths, and assorted pieces of scenery that might have to be flown onto the stage. (More than one actor has been clunked in the head by a flying piece of scenery.)

It's not possible to remove every safety hazard, but sets should, whenever possible, minimize the risks. The crew should be able to move them easily. And they should be placed so that people will not trip, fall, and break their legs.

Set Up and Strike

Opening night is approaching. The sets are built, and the painters are adding the final touches. What started as a pile of raw lumber has turned into beautiful scenery that will take the audience inside another world. There's just one problem: it's all still in the scene shop. Now, you have to figure out where it all goes and how to get it there.

Onward and Upward

If possible, put your sets onstage before they're completely built. What worked on paper might not work onstage. The size or scale may not translate into a bigger arena. The colors may wash out under the lights, or the lights may create an unwanted reflection or glare. That winding staircase may not fit through the stage door. It's a good idea to find out these problems as soon as possible so you have time to fix them.

This set fans out to provide multiple playing areas for the actors, as well as consistent good views for audience members who have different perspectives of the stage.

Hopefully, the stage manager has spiked the stage. This means that he or she has used special tape to mark the stage, showing where the sets and scenery will be placed.

Make sure that the crew knows how to move each set. Can one person handle it, or does it need two or more? If multiple people are needed, who takes the back and who takes the front? Make sure each crew member knows his or her position. From which side of the stage will it come? Does anything on the set need to change before it's moved? For example, if an actor's dramatic exit means he runs through the door and leaves it swinging open behind him, the crew needs to remember to shut the door before moving that set. Finally, establish the order in which things will happen and make sure the entire crew is aware of it.

Once these questions are answered, the stage manager can make a shift plot. This chart details who will do what during the scene changes. Although the actors have been rehearsing for weeks, the crew may only get a chance to fine-tune their efforts in the final week of rehearsal. The audience will not applaud like they do after the impressive dance number in the second act, but the crew's "dance" is just as important!

Sets can be moved on- and offstage in a number of ways. "Running" is the most common. This means that one or two people actually grab hold of the pieces (that's why they are sometimes called grips) and carry them into position. Heavy or awkward pieces might be mounted on castors (wheels) and can be rolled off.

A crew member spikes the stage with easily seen tape so that this table will be placed in the correct position each time.

Another way to move scenery is by "flying." In the theater, objects don't fly up and down; they fly "in" or "out." Flying scenery is handled by a separate crew who operates above the stage. Flown scenery has special requirements. It should have as few moving parts (such as a door or window) as possible. Otherwise, it might fall apart—perhaps on an actor's head!—while it's being moved.

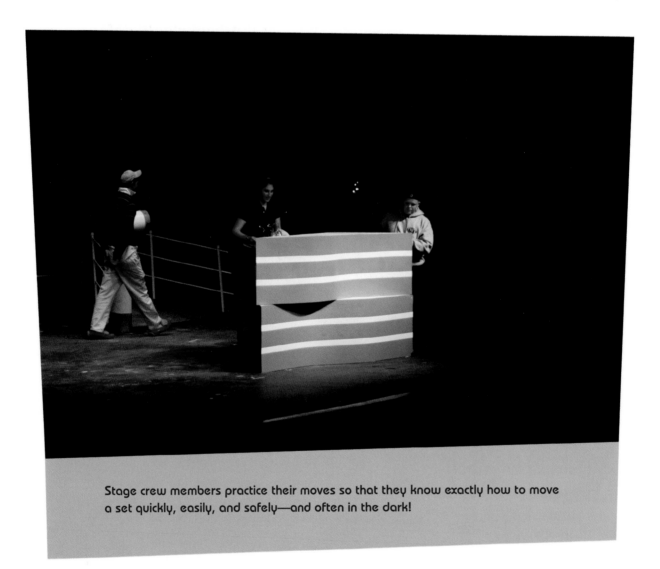

Stage crew members practice their moves so that they know exactly how to move a set quickly, easily, and safely—and often in the dark!

A Change in Scenery

Cue the final bang of the drum, dim the lights . . . Go! The few precious seconds between scenes are ticking away. For a major scene change, you might get half a minute.

If all goes according to plan, the running crew will be in the wings, waiting to make their entrance. Unlike actors' entrances, these will be quick and quiet. Dressed in dark clothing and sensible shoes, they go on, often working in pairs, to shift the set.

In recent times, there has been a trend toward "a vista" scene changes. This means that scene changes are not hidden from the audience, at least not entirely. Modern audiences often like to see this "behind-the-scenes" action. People will tolerate longer scene changes than if the stage was dark and they couldn't see anything. Changing a full set in thirty seconds takes perfectly timed movements. Watching a competent stage crew at work is like watching a mini-show itself.

Sometimes, a scene change starts even before the previous scene has ended. This is tempting to do if there is a long or tricky change coming up. In some cases, it can work. However, the action of the play and the attention of the audience are more important. Be sure scene changes do not interfere with the show. For example, suppose there is a chase scene that carries the actors to stage right. You might think a scene change at stage left would not interrupt the action. Although it may not physically interfere, it could distract the audience. Instead of watching the chase scene, they're watching the set change.

Finally, make sure the change fits the mood of the show. In *Technical Theater for Nontechnical People*, author Drew Campbell tells about a show where a casket is flown offstage after a funeral.

From Ship to Stage

Curtain down? In ancient Rome, the show began when the stage curtain was dropped, not raised. This changed during the Italian Renaissance, when theater crews were often made up of sailors. The idea of lifting the curtain came from them. They used the same methods they'd used on ships. The complex system of ropes and pipes used to fly scenery was known as rigging—just like on sailboats.

The tradition of not whistling backstage also comes from sailing. On ships, sailors whistled as a way to communicate with each other while they were scuttling around up in the rigging. Random whistling from below could send the wrong message and cause a disaster!

The audience started to laugh at the idea of the deceased going straight off to heaven. The somber mood was destroyed.

Sustainable Theater

Sets are not like cars, couches, or clothing. They are not usually meant to be used again and again. Traditionally, scenery had to last only for the run of one show.

But building new sets for every play isn't good for the environment. It's hard to justify using tons of lumber for such a short-lived purpose.

Also, many materials used to build and decorate sets are not environmentally friendly. Paint and glue often contain harsh chemicals that can pollute the water. Their fumes may be dangerous to the people who use them. Foams and plastics are made from petroleum, which is not a renewable resource. Also, they take a long time to break down, so they use up landfill space.

Shadowed soldiers fight behind the spotlighted figure of Napoleon Bonaparte in this production about the famous French military leader. A wash of red light adds to the violent mood.

Some people believe in the idea of sustainable theater. They want to do things that save natural resources. Set designers can work to design and build sets so that they can be reused in the future. Designers can also network with other theaters or drama groups to borrow existing sets.

Another solution is to use "green" products. These are easy to clean up and will not contaminate water. You can also use renewable or recycled material. However, these can have downsides, too. For example, suppose you need to cover a large flat with paper. Traditionally, you might use paper from a wide roll. You could use

A Bit Part

The performers' job is to perform the play, and the stage crew's job is to move the sets on and off. Right?

Well, sometimes.

Occasionally, a set change is particularly complicated or rushed. It seems there won't be enough crew members to get it done. What to do?

One option is to enlist the actors. This rarely happens at the professional level because the actors' contracts do not allow them to do extra work. Also, actors have their own jobs. They must remember their lines and movements, and they must stay in character. They may not be dressed appropriately to move scenery. Or, they may have a costume change before their next scene. However, actors with smaller parts, or chorus members, can often help.

Another idea is to turn the crew into actors. In *The Perfect Stage Crew*, author John Kaluta tells the story of dressing his *Guys and Dolls* crew up as waiters. They went onstage to begin cleaning up a restaurant set while the principal actors were finishing the scene.

recycled white office paper instead. However, although you are not using brand-new paper, it will take more glue to stick it to the flat.

Set building will be affected by time, money, and environmental concerns. It may mean that fewer sets are built. They may be a little bit smaller and a little bit simpler.

But imagination is a powerful thing. A good set designer uses his or her own creativity to inspire the audience. With this influence, a simple stroke of the paintbrush can be a stroke of genius. It won't matter whether the sets are rolled, dropped, flown, or simply dreamed—the audience will be transported right along with them.

GLOSSARY

apron The part of a proscenium stage that extends beyond the opening.

a vista In sight of the audience.

break points The places where a set comes apart.

CAD (computer-aided drawing) Technology that allows drawing using computers.

color palette A group of colors chosen to work together.

cyclorama A large, neutral-colored surface that covers the back of the stage.

downstage The part of the stage that is closer to the audience.

elevation A drawing that shows a set from the front.

flat A common type of set that is large and almost flat, like a painting.

flies The upper workings of a theater, from where scenery is lowered and lifted.

ground plan A bird's-eye view drawing of the stage showing placement of sets.

in-the-round A stage that allows for seating all around it.

minimalist design A style that uses few sets and relies on audience imagination.

opaque Unable to be seen through.

periaktoi A three-sided panel that can be turned to show different scenes.

proscenium A type of stage that resembles an open box overlooking the audience.

rendering A drawing that shows the stage and sets in perspective.

renewable Material that can be grown or manufactured easily.

rigging The system of cables, ropes, pipes, pulleys, and other equipment used to fly scenery.

scrim A type of cloth that is partially transparent or opaque, depending on lighting.

spike To tape the stage to show where sets will be placed.

stage left/right The sides of the stage from the actor's perspective.

stock scenery Sets that are kept in a theater's inventory to be reused.

strobe A rapidly pulsing light.

sustainable Maintainable or able to be continued for a long time.

thrust A type of stage that protrudes into the audience.

trap An opening in the stage floor that allows scenery to be lowered beneath the stage.

upstage The part of the stage that is farther from the audience.

virtual reality Computer technology that creates realistic situations.

wagon A rolling platform used to move scenery or sets.

Arts, Crafts & Theater Safety (ACTS)
181 Thompson Street, #23
New York, NY 10012-2586
(212) 777-0062
E-mail: ACTSNYC@cs.com
Web site: http://www.artscraftstheatersafety.org
ACTS is a nonprofit organization that provides health and safety
    information and advice to theater and other arts communities.

Canada Council for the Arts
350 Albert Street
P.O. Box 1047
Ottawa, ON K1P 5V8
Canada
(800) 263-5588 or (613) 566-4414
Web site: http://www.canadacouncil.ca/theatre
This organization's theater section helps to create and distribute plays,
    and offers financial assistance.

Canadian Institute for Theatre Technology
340-207 Bank Street
Ottawa, ON K2P 2N2
Canada
(613) 482-1165 or (888) 271-3383
E-mail: info@citt.org
Web site: http://www.citt.org

This organization helps its members through education and professional development, and promotes live performance in Canada.

National Arts Centre of Canada
P.O. Box 1534, Stn B
Ottawa, ON K1P 5W1
Canada
(613) 947-7000 or (866) 850-ARTS
E-mail: info@nac-cna.ca
Web site: http://www.nac-cna.ca/en/index.cfm
This organization stages performances in a variety of areas, including music, dance, and theater, and works to promote the arts through education.

Set Decorators Society of America
1646 N. Cherokee Avenue
Hollywood, CA 90028
(323) 462-3060
E-mail: sdsa@setdecorators.org
Web site: http://www.setdecorators.org/incEngine
This organization provides resources for set decorators and publishes a quarterly magazine.

U.S. Institute for Theatre Technology, Inc. (USITT)
315 South Crouse Avenue, Suite 200
Syracuse, NY 13210
(315) 463-6463 or (800) 938-7488
E-mail: info@office.usitt.org
Web site: http://www.usitt.org/index.html

USITT works to promote education and communication among people working in performing arts design and technology.

Web Sites

Due to the changing nature of Internet links, Rosen Publishing has developed an online list of Web sites related to the subject of this book. This site is updated regularly. Please use this link to access the list:

http://www.rosenlinks.com/hsm/scen

Campbell, Drew. *Technical Theater for Nontechnical People.* New York, NY: Allworth Press, 2004.

Carter, Paul, and George Chiang. *Backstage Handbook: An Illustrated Almanac of Technical Information.* Louisville, KY: Broadway Press, 1994.

Davies, Gill. *Stage Source Book: Sets.* London, England: A&C Black Publishers Limited, 2004.

Friedman, Lise. *Break a Leg! The Kids' Guide to Acting and Stagecraft.* New York, NY: Workman Publishing Company, 2002.

Ionazzi, Daniel. *The Stagecraft Handbook.* Cincinnati, OH: Betterway Books, 1996.

Lawler, Mike. *Careers in Technical Theater.* New York, NY: Allworth Press, 2007.

Raoul, Bill. *Stock Scenery Construction Handbook.* Louisville, KY: Broadway Press, 1999.

Schumacher, Thomas, and Jeff Kurtti. *How Does the Show Go On?* New York, NY: Disney Editions, 2007.

BIBLIOGRAPHY

Bachanov, Arlene. "Croswell Alumnus Returns as Titanic Set Designer." *Daily Telegram* (Adrian, MI), June 9, 2008. Retrieved June 22, 2008 (http://www.lenconnect.com/ archive/x710597999/Croswell-alumnus-returns-as-Titanic-set-designer).

Blood, Melanie. "Set Designer." State University of New York–Geneseo. Course Materials, Theatre 140. Fall 2007. Retrieved June 23, 2008 (http://www.geneseo.edu/~blood/ SetDesign1.html).

Blurton, John. *Scenery: Drafting and Construction*. New York, NY: Routledge, 2001.

Campbell, Drew. *Technical Theater for Nontechnical People*. New York, NY: Allworth Press, 2004.

Crabtree, Susan, and Peter Beudert. *Scenic Art for the Theatre: History, Tools, and Techniques*. Woburn, MA: Butterworth-Heinemann, 1998.

Fried, Larry K., and Theresa J. May. *Greening Up Our Houses: A Guide to a More Ecologically Sound Theatre*. New York, NY: Drama Book Publishers, 1994.

Kaluta, John. *The Perfect Stage Crew*. New York, NY: Allworth Press, 2003.

Kenrick, John. *The Complete Idiot's Guide to Amateur Theatricals*. New York, NY: Penguin Group, Inc., 2006.

Lee, Robert L. *Everything About Theatre!* Colorado Springs, CO: Meriwether Publishing, Ltd., 1996.

Orton, Keith. *Model-Making for the Stage*. Ramsbury, England: The Crowood Press, Ltd., 2004.

Reaney, Mark. "Art in Real-Time: Theatre and Virtual Reality."
Séminaire CIREN, Université Paris 8. March 24, 2000.
Retrieved July 10, 2008 (http://web.ku.edu/~mreaney/
reaney/ciren).

Rich, Frank. "Critic's Notebook: How Set Design Can Bolster or
Sabotage, and 2 Heroes of the Art." NYTimes.com, January 18,
1990. Retrieved June 23, 2008 (http://query.nytimes.com/
gst/fullpage.html?res=9C0CE2D91E3FF93BA25752C0
A966958260).

Rossol, Monona. *The Health and Safety Guide for Film, TV, and
Theater.* New York, NY: Allworth Press, 2000.

Rupke Van Farowe, Roxanne. "Behind the Scenes: Light, Costume,
and Set Designers Enhance Calvin Theater." Spark Online
Edition, Summer 2000. Retrieved June 21, 2008 (http://www.
calvin.edu/publications/spark/sum00/feature3.htm).

Sommer, Elyse. "Set Designer Derek McLane." CurtainUp.com.
Retrieved August 24, 2008 (http://64.233.167.104/search?q=
cache:XSjXQxBRFY8J:www.curtainup.com/mclane.html).

Thorne, Gary. *Stage Design: A Practical Guide.* Ramsbury, England:
The Crowood Press, Ltd., 1999.

Winslow, Colin. *The Handbook of Set Design.* Ramsbury, England:
The Crowood Press, Ltd., 2006.

INDEX

About the Author

Diane Bailey acted and sang in several of her high school's musicals. She never had the lead, so she spent a lot of time hanging out with the stage crew. Since then, she has always found backstage to be just as much fun as onstage. She has two children and writes on a variety of nonfiction topics.

Photo Credits

Cover (background), pp. 1, 15, 19, 27, 29, 30–31, 34, 37, 43, 46, 47, 48 © Michael McGarty; cover (inset) © www.istockphoto.com/ Claude Dagenais; pp. 4–5 © AP Images; p. 8 © Elliott Franks/ ArenaPAL/Topham/The Image Works; p. 9 Mary Knox Merrill/*The Christian Science Monitor*/Getty Images; pp. 12–13 Colin Willoughby/ ArenaPAL © ArenaPal/Topham/The Image Works; p. 17 © Bob Daemmrich/The Image Works; pp. 22–23 © Eastcott-Momatiuk/The Image Works; pp. 40–41 © Jeff Greenberg/The Image Works; p. 51 © ArenaPal/Topham/The Image Works.

Designer: Sam Zavieh; Editor: Bethany Bryan
Photo Researcher: Cindy Reiman